The Righteous Women Bring Moshiach

A collection of translated quotes and adaptations of talks and letters of the Rebbe King Moshiach Shlita

As well as essays expounding on the above

Published and Copyrighted By

Living Moshiach Publications
RebbeMessiahLives.770@gmail.com
www.LivingMoshiach.com

5775 (2015)

Content

Dvar Malchus

Dvar Malchus Bo-Beshalach, 5752
(adaptation)

About the greatness of the Jewish women and girls, may they live, of our generation

The Righteousness of the Women

The Rebbe Rayatz was devoted to the education of Jewish women and girls, through emphasizing their unique quality; that they are the mainstay of the house and they affect the entire household.

The greatness of the women is apparent from the beginning of Jewish history.

At Matan Torah, Hashem told Moshe to teach the women first. Even more significant, the women refused to give their jewelry for the making of the golden calf, which is the opposite of Matan Torah.

In the donations for the Mishkan, the women were the first to donate (and happily donated the jewelry that they refused to contribute towards the golden calf). The quality of their donations was also exceptional: they wove the goat hair while it was still attached to the live goats, a special skill making the finished product brighter and of a higher quality.

The Jews were redeemed from Egypt in the merit of the righteous women. So too our generation, the first generation of the ultimate Redemption, is redeemed in the merit of the righteous women. Our generation is actually a reincarnation of the generation that left Egypt, so the women of our generation are those same women in whose merit we were redeemed. Moreover, also in the Redemption, the special quality of women stand out – the virtue of receivers is revealed in the Redemption.

Yahrtzeits of the Rebbetzins

The Yahrtzeit of the Rebbe Rayatz (Rabbi Yosef Yitzchak) is at the same time of year as the Yahrtzeits of Rebbetzins: his grandmother, Rebbetzin Rivkah (Yud Shvat); his mother, Rebbetzin Shterna Sarah (13 Shvat); and his daughter, Rebbetzin Chaya Mushkah (22 Shvat). The Ma'amar that the Rebbe Rayatz gave to learn on Yud Shvat – "Basi Legani Achosi Kalah" ("I have entered My garden") speaks about the Jewish People, the "wife" of Hashem and their accomplishment in bringing holiness down into the world. Within the Jewish People, this is especially expressed by the women.

Shabbos Candles: G-dly Light

The Rebbe Rayatz (Rabbi Yosef Yitzchak) passed away in the year 5710 (1950) on Shabbos the Parshah of Bo, when Hashem took Moshe to the holy source of Paroh – the level at which all the G-dly lights burst forth (see the previous Sicha). The Rebbe Rayatz worked his whole life to light up the world with the G-dly light of Torah and Mitzvos. This is especially connected to the Jewish women, who light Shabbos and Yom Tov candles which usher in Shabbos for the whole family and represent the culmination of the work during the week.

The ultimate revelation of all the G-dly lights is in the true and complete Redemption.

With Tambourines

The next Parshah, Beshalach, also expresses the greatness of the women. It speaks about the song the Jews sang to thank Hashem for splitting the Yam Suf. The women celebrated with greater joy than the men – accompanying their rejoicing with tambourines. They had so much certainty that Hashem would make miracles and redeem them that they prepared tambourines even while still in Egypt.

Miriam, who led the women in their jubilation, epitomizes the extra joy over the redemption. When she was born, the exile became more bitter – but the redemption came through this bitterness. Miriam brought about the redemption of Moshe, as well as the ultimate Redemption through Moshiach (a descendant of Miriam).

Miriam suffered bitterly in the Golus, and this bitterness caused the redemption. She prophesized that Moshe would be born and would save the Jewish People, and she bitterly and impatiently waited until her prophecy would be fulfilled.

When the Egyptians drowned in the Yam Suf – the completion of the redemption – Miriam led the women's celebration, accompanied by tambourines. Because she suffered so bitterly in the exile, her joy at the redemption was very great.

The Lessons from Devorah

The Haftorah of Beshalach is the song of Devorah, a woman. Devorah would make wicks for the Menorah in the Mishkan, which gave light to the whole world. Similarly, every Jewish woman lights Shabbos candles in her home, a miniature Mishkan, and these lights also light up the whole world. Devorah was also careful about Tznius – the foundation of the Jewish People – as seen from the fact that she sat under a palm tree so as not to come to a situation of Yichud, because a palm tree doesn't have shade.

Through following in the ways of Devorah, the righteous women of our generation bring the ultimate peace in Eretz Yisroel in the true and complete Redemption, just as Devorah brought peace to the land for forty years.

Instructions for this Time

The days of the Yahrtzeits of the Rebbetzins are a fitting time to strengthen our following in the ways of the Rebbetzins. This way they will live through us, and more than that, they will be literally alive through their coming back to life in the Resurrection.

The following is a quote from the Sicha:

"Just as at the Exodus from Egypt 'the righteous women…were certain that Hashem will make miracles for them, and they took tambourines out of Egypt,' so too regarding the Redemption from this last exile, that the Jewish righteous women…are certain that literally immediately the true and complete Redemption comes, to the extent that they begin singing* with tambourines and dances, for the coming of the true and complete Redemption!"

It is important to note the Rebbe Melech HaMoshiach Shlita adds in a footnote that the singing should be "with the height of modesty, obviously, as the lesson from Devorah".

Together with davening that Hashem should bring the Geulah immediately, and screaming bitterly "Until when?!" the righteous women are mainly permeated with strong happiness expressed in song, about the coming of Moshiach, that "here he (the King Moshiach) comes" and has already come!

Immediately we will sing the "tenth song" in the true and complete Redemption!

Dvar Malchus Chof-Beis Shvat, 5752
(adaptation)

The 22nd Day of Shvat

The Rebbetzin's Yahrtzeit is on the 22nd of Shvat, the 11th month. The number eleven represents a level above creation – higher than the ten Sefiros with which Hashem created the world. 22 is double eleven. The 22nd day of Shvat represents the complete revelation of the level of eleven. This revelation includes two aspects (double) of eleven: 1) "eleven" as it elevates "ten" (the world) and 2) "eleven" as it is on its own – Hashem's Essence.

The Name Chaya Mushka

The name Chaya Mushka expresses the unification of Hashem's Essence and the world. "Chaya" is life – both the life which enlivens and is contained within the person (the body as well as the ten "soul powers" – the Sefiros) and the life which transcends and encompasses the person (the level of the "encompassing powers" – will and pleasure). "Chaya" mainly refers to the life within the person. "Mushka" – fragrance – represents the level transcending and encompassing the person (the Neshamah has pleasure from fragrance – different from food which goes inside the body).

Both of these names combined in one person represents the revelation of the Neshamah's Essence (above the person) becoming internalized within the person.

Indeed, the passing of Rebbetzin Chaya Mushka marked the completion of the last stage of preparing the world for the Geulah (in making a dwelling for Hashem below).

Women Make a Beautiful Home for Hashem

Hashem created the world because He desired to have a home for His Essence in this physical world. Every part of a home and everything in a home is there to serve its owner. More than that, the ultimate home is one that is not only functional but also beautiful.

Women make their homes beautiful both physically and spiritually. Women are beautiful and are able to make things beautiful. They have spiritual beauty which is expressed in this world in physical beauty. This is because women have an integral part in making a beautiful home for Hashem. We see this especially in the three special Mitzvos which were given to women:

1) Shabbos and Yom Tov candles add visible physical and spiritual light and beauty to the home.

2) Women are responsible for the Mitzvah of taking off Challah and Kashrus in general. Kosher foods positively affect a person's nature, because food becomes a part of the person.

3) Taharas Hamishpachah makes the family pure and beautiful, as well as physically and spiritually healthy.

In addition, the mother is responsible for the education – the foundation for life – of her children. The younger the children are, the more dependent they are on their mother. From the earliest age, she permeates them with Yiddishkeit – with a Jewish woman's characteristic gentleness and love. This foundation leads them to do Torah and Mitzvos in a beautiful way. One example is the good custom of mothers to sing to their babies that Torah is the best, sweetest, most beautiful thing. This gives them love for Torah and Mitzvos that remains with them even when they grow old.

A home should have "Chaya" – liveliness and "Mushka" – fragrance. This is important also in Hashem's "home" in this world, which we create through Torah and Mitzvos. This gives the Owner – Hashem – pleasure from His home.

Instructions

We should strengthen our performance of the three women's Mitzvos, including that even little girls should light a Shabbos candle once they are able to understand. (They should light before the mother so the mother can help them.) We should also influence others in these Mitzvos. This is in addition to the special Service of our time to accept Moshiach and actually bring the Geulah for all the generations.

We should make our homes places of Torah, davening and kindness, like a Bais Hamikdash. Each child should have his or her own Chumash, Siddur, Pushka and Tanya in his/her room.

We should strengthen the education of children, starting with the smallest ones.

We should spread Yiddishkeit and Chassidus – especially the Shluchos (the Shluchos convention is held close to the Rebbetzin's Yahrtzeit).

We receive the power for all of this from 770 Bais Moshiach – a place of Torah, davening and kindness.

We should tell women about their great merit to bring the Redemption. And the main thing is that the true and complete Redemption should come – in the merit of the righteous women!

Womens' Mitzvos Bring The Redemption

"...In addition to the fact that all Jews have a mission from Hashem to make a dwelling for Hashem in the lowest realms (as spoken many times at length), Jewish women and daughters have a special mission to make it that it should be a "nice dwelling" with "nice vessels,"

Beginning with the fulfillment and the strengthening of the three above-mentioned Mitzvos which were especially given to them in their personal homes, Kosher eating and drinking, family purity, and holy Shabbos and Holiday candles, including – the efforts that also little girls (when they are capable of understanding) should light these candles (before their mother, in order that the mother can help them etc.).

And likewise – may they succeed to influence other Jewish daughters and girls that they should also fulfill and strengthen these mentioned Mitzvos...

Including and mainly – in the present time, the last moments before the Redemption – to arouse oneself as well as all Jewish women and daughters regarding the great merit of Jewish women and daughters to bring the true and complete Redemption *literally* immediately, which comes "in the merit of the Righteous women that are in the generation,"..."

(Excerpt from Dvar Malchus 22nd of Shevat, 5752 – free translation)

Remedy for Infertility, Segulah to Have Children

The three Mitzvos that were (mainly) given to women are Kosher food and drink, family purity and Shabbos and Holiday candle lighting. These three Mitzvos are alluded to in the name ChaNaH: taking off **Ch**alah (Kosher food and drink), **N**iddah (family purity) and **H**adlakas Haner (lighting Shabbos and Holiday candles).

Keeping these Mitzvos and influencing other women to do the same this is a Segulah to have children (remedy for infertility) – just as Chanah miraculously had children although she originally was not capable.

Strengthening the fulfillment of these Mitzvos along with the other Mitzvos will bring Hashem to send Moshiach to redeem us and lead us upright to our Land.

Free adaptation of an excerpt of the address of the 2nd day of Rosh Hashanah 5739 (1979)

The Blessing of the Revelation of Moshiach

Our Sages relate a story of how a husband and wife prayed for rain and the rain came mainly in merit of the wife's prayers. Women are the main ones who make Hashem a physical dwelling in this world – educating the children and conducting the home in general in accordance with the will of Hashem. And the verse says, "when you will heed My laws... I shall give you rain its time."

Rain is the source of all blessings. Indeed, when there is the G-dly Service of the Jewish people in general and in every Jewish home in particular, namely, the G-dly Service of the "foundation of the home" – the wife – educating the children and conducting the home in general, then all the blessings are attained, "your wife is fruitful as a vine, your children are like olive shoots [seated] around your table," children blessed by Hashem, the "army of Hashem" who will greet Moshiach, and will rejoice upon the salvation of Hashem.

Adapted from Likkutei Sichos vol. 9, pg. 397 ff.

The Strong Influence of Woman

Jewish women have to be occupied in illuminating every place with Torah and Mitzvos, and on the contrary, in many matters the influence of women is greater than that of the men – only that their efforts must be done with the height of modesty, in a truly scrupulous manner, a self understood. (Excerpt from an Address in 5747 – adaptation)

We must all think deeply into the great responsibility of a woman, and the most important role which she has in insuring the good and fortune of her husband and family,
As Shlomo Hamelech says (Mishlei 14, 1): Chachmas Nashim – smart conduct of women – Bansah Beisah – builds the beauty of her house; the opposite scenario, is Heaven forbid as the Posuk says there following the above.
With blessings to every one of you, and with special wishes for success in your work and in your own individual matters.
Adaptation from a letter on the 2nd day of Rosh Chodesh Tammuz,
5713

Women and the Emunah that the Rebbe King Moshiach Shlita is Alive

A collection of excerpts from Sichos of the Rebbe King Moshiach Shlita

Emunah

The women are first at Matan Torah - having no part in the Aigel! A lesson for our times.

Dvar Malchus "Concerning the advantage of the Jewish women and daughters, may they live, of our generation" – 5752 (ch. 1) [adaptation]: Hashem told Moshe to speak to the women first at the giving of the Torah. Additionally and mainly – the women did not give their gold to make the Aigel. They did not take part in the sin of the Aigel, which was the opposite of the giving of the Torah!

Likkutei Sichos vol. 8 pg. 315 ff. [adaptation]:

Indeed the women withstood the great test[1] that not all the men were able to withstand – they did not take part in the sin of the Aigel! The reason for this is that the concept of Emunah in women is much stronger than in men. The whole Jewish religion is built on Emunah – belief. True, one must understand as much as possible; however, first and foremost and "at the end of the day" there is the feeling of Emunah – a feeling that cannot be shaken or tampered by questions or tests. This feeling in women has its full effect on their daily lives. In our time also, one must not be intimidated by questions or obstacles. Rather, we go with firmness and the strength of Emunah, which becomes the guide and illuminator in all times through our fulfillment of Torah and Mitzvos. This conduct brings the illuminated world through Moshiach.

Alive!

The Rebbe King Moshiach Shlita lives in a physical body in 770 – Beis Moshiach, and continues to do everything he did in the past years (e.g. Sunday dollars etc.)!

In Dvar Malchus Bo 5752 the Rebbe King Moshiach Shlita explains that the previous leaders of the generations passed away since Hashem revealed Himself to them. Since a soul in a body could not handle such a great revelation, they passed away (like at Matan Torah). This was because the physicality was not yet refined and therefore unable to accept this great

---

[1] *[And did not think that Moshe passed away.]*

Revelation. The innovation of our generation is that the leader does not pass away, for the physical body can now accept this great Revelation – the physicality is now refined; as we see that the non-Jews help the Jews serve Hashem.

The following is a quote (free translation) from that Sicha. (ch. 13) – "... The novelty of our generation – the ninth [the Rebbe King Moshiach Shlita] over all the previous generations, even the generation before this one (the eigth generation [the Rebbe Rayatz]): since the Redemption did not come then in actuality the "Bo El Paraoh" (the revelation of the "bursting forth of all the Lights [of Hashem]" below) was not at the height of perfection as a soul in a healthy body (there was the histalkus [leaving] of the soul from the body and even the soul in a body was in a situation that "the speech was in exile" etc.), this is not so in our generation – the last generation of Golus and first generation of Geulah..."

In Dvar Malchus Shoftim 5751 the Rebbe King Moshiach Shlita explains that there always must be a leader of the generation existing without change, not even the change of being buried – similar to the existence of the Even Hashsiah[2] without change (especially emphasized by the Rebbe King Moshiach Shlita whose leadership began in the year ה"שתי (5710)).The following is a quote (free translation) from that Sicha. (ch. 12) – "...Just as there is a judge and prophet in every generation, and this is of "the foundations of the religion", that always and everywhere there is revelation of G-dliness below,... As He reveals Himself amongst us through "a prophet I will appoint for them... like you" the Leader of the generation "who is everything" "the Tzadik is the foundation of the world",

---

[2] *The stone from which the world was founded.*

19

Similar to the Even Hashsiah – which is found in a specific place in this physical world and exists always without changes (not even the change of being buried, like the Aron which was buried and the like), similar to how a judge and prophet exist (eternally [without change]) in every generation (signifying the revelation of G- dliness in the world in a constant fashion)..."

In Dvar Malchus Tzav 5751 the Rebbe King Moshiach Shlita explains that true eternality is only when it is in all details. The following is a quote (free translation) from that Sicha. (Footnote 69) "For the complete idea of eternity is specifically when it is drawn and recognized in all the details, for even if one detail isn't eternal this shows a "weakness" even in the matters which are eternal, for there is place and possibility for the opposite of eternity."

In "Kuntres ... Beis Rabeinu Shebibavel" 5752 the Rebbe King Moshiach Shlita says that his majesty's permanent place is Beis Moshiach – 770.

(ch.5&6) "...And according to this we may explain the greatness of "Beis Rabeinu Shebibavel" – that since it is the permanent place (house) of the leader of the generation... the permanent place of "Beis Rabeinu"... until the coming of our righteous redeemer [when we will return to Yerushalayim]."

Celebrating "Moshiach has already come!"

The unique connection of women and the coming of Moshiach.

Dvar Malchus "Concerning the advantage of the Jewish women and daughters, may they live, of our generation" – 5752 (ch. 8) [adaptation]:

Just as at Yetzias Mitzrayim the righteous women were certain that Hashem would make miracles for them, so too women are rejoicing now through song with tambourines and dances (in a most modest manner). This is due to their great certainty that "behold this one (Moshiach) is coming" and has already come.

Dvar Malchus "B'cha Yivarech Yisroel" – 22nd of Shevat 5752 (ch. 16) [adaptation]: Women make a beautiful, vibrant, bright and fragrant dwelling place for Hashem below, especially through Shabbos candles (as well as their other Mitzvos of Kashrus and Taharas Hamishpachah (ibid ch. 14)) including the ultimate perfection of "the light of Moshiach" and "the air of Moshiach"* in the Geulah, which comes in the merit of the righteous women!

*) See Dvar Malchus Toldos 5752 (2) ch. 11. [The revelation of Moshiach's existence (liveliness) – as the King Moshiach is "the air of Moshiach." All the accomplishments of the Rebbe King Moshiach Shlita (revealing his majesty clearly to the whole world as Moshiach) and all the matters of the days of Moshiach, which we now see in the world are "the light of Moshiach." Indeed, the whole Redemption is an extension and outcome of Moshiach being here and alive with us just as a flame exists from the air around it. The announcement of "Long live our Master Teacher and Rebbe King Moshiach Forever" reveals the existence of the King Moshiach in the world.]

Women in the Dynasty of Moshiach - *Miriam*

Miriam brought about the redemption from Egypt (see below) as well as the ultimate Redemption, through being an ancestress of Moshiach in the merit of her saving the Jewish baby boys in Egypt.

Our sages tell us that before Moishe Rabbeinu (Mosses our teacher) was born, Miriam his sister would say by way of prophecy that her mother would give birth to a son, who would save the Jewish people. After Moishe Rabbeinu was born they hid him from the Egyptians. This was because they had decreed that every boy that was born must be thrown into the Nile River. When they couldn't hide the baby anymore, they were forced to send him away in the Nile River. Upon seeing this, Miriam's father spanked her lightly, on her head, saying "what has become of your prophecy". This is why it says in the verse "and his sister stood in the distance to see (what will happen to him)" – to see what will happen to her prophecy. The Rebbe King Moshiach Shlita elaborates on this in the address of Boi - Beshalach 5752 (1991): From then on, she impatiently anticipated the fulfillment of her prophecy. Therefore, when Moishe Rabbeinu redeemed the Jewish people from Egypt and the Egyptians were drowned in the ocean, she rejoiced immensely upon seeing the complete fulfillment of her prophecy. Miriam led the other women in a great celebration, even greater than the celebration of the men. His majesty ends that address by saying that similarly now women are already rejoicing, for they are certain that imminently we will see the true and complete redemption. This is because the main emphasis now, is not on yearning for the Redemption, but rather rejoicing the fact that behold "here he (Moshiach) has already come", to redeem us from this exile.

There is a very important lesson we should take from the above. Of course, we are not intimidated by anything that seemingly challenges the words of the Rebbe King Moshiach Shlita, our prophet. We are certain that his Majesty is alive physically in our midst, and is revealing the ultimate Redemption in this world - when the whole world will be transformed to good. [This can be seen especially in how the gentiles help the Jewish people in our times. Their good conduct is no comparison to their harsh decrees upon the Jewish people in the former times, as in the Egyptian exile.] However, in addition to our assurance, we should be truthfully happy about this.

The Rebbe King Moshiach Shlita says that the only thing left is for G-d Almighty to open our eyes. We will then see the true and complete Redemption and we will truly rejoice without any boundaries.

"Moshe is True and his Torah is True"

Story translated and adapted with permission from "Vayikahalu El HaMelech" II, Explanation by Rabbi Eliyahu Yonah Benyaminson

Ev'yasar Ben-Or relates the following story: "In the Yishuv Keren in the Holy Land, lives a traditional Jewish couple, which lately encountered persistent arguments between each other. The situation became so severe that they decided to get divorced.

"On Sunday the 9th of Marcheshvan 5768, I met the husband who painfully related his situation. I gave him a dollar that I received from the Rebbe King Moshiach Shlita during the month of Tishrei, that year. I told him that the dollar is a supernatural blessing for all things. When he got home he placed the dollar on the table in the living room, without telling his wife about it.

"That night his wife dreamt that she saw the Rebbe King Moshiach Shlita who told her that 'a good wife fulfills the will of her husband!' She awoke startled; however, she didn't ascribe much importance to the dream.

"In the course of the following day, while her husband was out, she suddenly noticed the dollar which was on the table. Without understanding why, she suddenly felt an ambiance of holiness. She immediately covered her hair, (she generally was accustomed to cover hair, only when she went outside). When her husband came home, she asked him: 'where is this dollar from?'

"'This is a dollar that was received from the Rebbe King Moshiach Shlita!' he answered. She was momentarily rendered speechless. 'Just last night I dreamt of him!' she said with excitement, and told him about her dream.

"It's unnecessary to mention that they completely abandoned any thought of getting divorced..."

&&&&

This story expresses a very important point: the fact that the Rebbe Melech HaMoshiach Shlita is alive as a soul in a body literally, is intrinsically connected to the complete fulfillment of Torah and Mitzvos. The dollar that the Rebbe Melech HaMoshiach Shlita gave recently brought her to cover her hair.

The Rebbe Melech HaMoshiach Shlita explains the connection of these two as follows: Moshe Rabeinu is intrinsically connected to the Torah, "Moshe is true and his Torah is true." (As the Talmud relates that on Rosh Chodesh in the desert near the place where the group of Korach was swallowed up in the earth one can hear the group of Korach saying "Moshe is true and his Torah is true") True means that it is eternal. What shows that something is truly eternal – when it remains eternal (without change) even as it is clothed in this physical world where everything undergoes change. Both Moshe and the Torah are eternal. The Torah even as it descended into this world it does not change – every aspect of it (its laws etc.) apply at all times. Similarly Moshe is always alive: the Neshamah of Moshe is clothed in a physical body – in the body of the leader of every generation, as our sages say "there must always be a Moshe (of the generation) in whom the Nesahmah of Moshe is clothed." Moshe is eternal because he is connected to the Torah that is eternal.

One of the reasons for the fact that the Rebbe King Moshiach Shlita is alive physically is because he is the Moshe of the generation. Since there must always be a Moshe of the generation alive as a soul in a body and the Rebbe King Moshiach Shlita has said many times that our generation is the last generation of exile and first of Redemption, indeed he is the final and ultimate leader (Moshe of the generation). The more this fact is emphasized the more the keeping of Torah and Mitzvos – in our modern day of age – is as it should be.

Some Instructions Regarding Birth

From the words of the Rebbe King Moshiach Shlita

Adapted and complied by Rabbi Eliyahu Yonah Benyaminson

✍ Right after a baby is born they clean the baby and wrap the baby in a clean cloth; this helps the baby be strong, etc. The lesson from this that after we do service of leaving Egypt, our limitations, and we resolve to Daven well etc., notwithstanding the possible hardships we must enter a Sukkah (as Hashem made for us when we left Egypt), namely an encompassing Service (like the clean cloth they wrap the baby with), which the Sukkah is an encompassing revelation that affects us also in an internal fashion. (Possible examples of this: hanging on the crib a picture of the Rebbe Melech Hamoshiach Shlita, Shir Hamaalos, Moshiach flag, Yechi sign).

✍ The conduct of the mother during her pregnancy affects the baby in her womb, which therefore, it is the custom of righteous women to add more stringencies and be more scrupulous in the fulfillment of Torah and Mitzvos during their pregnancy for the good of the baby – things the babies hear or see even during the pregnancy affect the baby. Moreover, even prior to their pregnancy as known regarding being careful when leaving the Mikvah.

✍ It is important to strengthen the custom to have a Shir Ham'alos etc. hanging in the room of the mother and the baby, immediately when the mother comes to the hospital, during the preparations for the birth, and most certainly during the birth itself as well as after the birth. (Sometimes the Shir Hama'alos must be covered with a double covering – consult a rabbi). If necessary one should explain to the hospital staff that this will calm the mother and thereby ease the birth and simplify the efforts of the doctor.

✍ Due to medical reasons women today give birth in a hospital and not at home. Being that it is for medical reasons it is (in accordance with) the instruction of the Torah that a doctor has the ability and empowerment to heal.

The Moshiach Method

B.F. from Kfar Chabad has given birth to two children (may Hashem bless her with many more) and shares how to experience birth for what it truly is: a miniature Redemption.

Focusing on Moshiach while giving birth is the best-working pain reliever, and has no side effects. Here are some tips that will help you prepare for and get through birth in a happy, Moshiach-focused way – a taste of the time when Hashem will take away the pain from birth.

• A general tip in all aspects of life: Learn the Sichos of Dvar Malchus regularly. As you learn, apply the messages of the Sichos to your life. Think about how the words of the Rebbe King Moshiach Shlita are expressed in your marriage, family, etc.

An example that has to do with birth: In the Dvar Malchus of Bo, the Rebbe King Moshiach Shlita talks about a level at which all G-dly lights burst forth. When we think about how this is expressed in a woman's life, birth is definitely an intense G- dly experience. A G-dly Neshamah is entering the world. Along with the most intense pain, it is also the most intense joy.

• Learn well or memorize the parts of the Sichos that talk about how the Rebbe King Moshiach Shlita lives forever, that the time of the Redemption has arrived, etc. With each contraction, focus on one of these ideas.

• Before giving birth, look at many pictures of the Rebbe King Moshiach Shlita, and visualize them during contractions.

• Scream "Yechi!" Screaming helps ease the pain of labor. In the Egyptian exile, the Jewish women were afraid to scream while giving birth because of the decree that the baby boys be thrown into the Nile. Hashem punished them for this with the plague of frogs, which make a lot of noise. "Yechi" is the best thing to scream – it will help you focus on Moshiach, which will ease your pain much more than regular screaming, and will also spread the awareness of Moshiach to the hospital staff and others around you. You can also say "Y echi" to distract yourself when the nurse inserts the IV, etc., and then explain to her what it means.

• From birth, B.F. puts a baby hat with "Yechi" written on it – a baby "Yechi Yarmulke" – on her baby boys' heads.

May Hashem bless all of us to give birth to many healthy children, with wonderful birth experiences, and mainly – may we see the Rebbe King Moshiach Shlita who will bring the true and complete Redemption immediately!

Avoiding Yichud Brings the Geulah and is Characteristic of the Geulah

Compiled by Rabbi Eliyahu Yonah Benyaminson

"**...And we may add an additional point in the relation of "Devorah's date-palm" to the state of the Time to Come – in correlation with the words of our Sages "why specifically under a date-palm... because of the prohibition of Yichud (since "under a date-palm" it is not possible to be secluded [for it doesn't have any shade]), and we may say that this alludes to the fact, that the "seclusion" of the Jewish people (who are compared to bees (Devorah)) is only with Hashem alone, and therefore we must avoid situations of Yichud to the utmost degree ("under a date-palm"), and through this we merit the seclusion [unification] of the Jewish people with Hashem in** the Time to Come ("in the Days of Moshiach will be the marriage [of the Jewish people with Hashem]")..."

(Dvar Malchus 15th of Shevat 5752, ch. 7)

Moshiach Makes Sure the Jewish People "Avoid Situations of Yichud"

The Rebbe King Moshiach Shlita made a specific request to the authors of a known encyclopedic work Otzar Haposkim to publicize an arousal regarding common cases of Yichud which people might have not realized are a problem. They printed this letter of the Rebbe King Moshiach Shlita in vol. 9 of their work. **Indeed, the Rebbe King Moshiach Shlita – the one who actually brings the Time to Come, makes sure the Jewish people "avoid situations of Yichud to the utmost degree"!**

Some Laws of Yichud

Based on Sichos and a Letter of the Rebbe King Moshiach Shlita

- **Even a parent of an adopted child with their adopted child are not permitted to be in a secluded place (if they are opposite gender) and similarly a stepparent with their spouse's child. [Likewise, they are prohibited to hug or**

kiss their adopted child (if they are opposite gender).]
- **The prohibition of Yichud applies in a car. For example, a girl may not go in a car with a male driver, or vice versa.**

Women's Modesty Brings "Eternal Peace" in the Geulah

"[In the beginning of the Haftorah it says] "And she would sit under 'Devorah's date-palm,'" "why specifically under a date-palm... because of [the prohibition of] Yichud" ("for it is tall and it doesn't have shade (it has no branches towards the bottom of it) and no one can be secluded there with her as in a house") – the virtue of *modesty* ("the true honor of the king's daughter *is her modesty*"), ... which this is the foundation upon which every Jewish house stands.

And based on this we may explain also the culmination of the Haftorah "and the land was quiet for forty years," ... which alludes to the fact that through the conduct of the Jewish righteous women in the footsteps of Devorah, we merit the phenomenon of "the land was quiet," including the ultimate perfection of "the land was quiet," with the entering into the complete Eretz Yisroel (a land of ten nations) in the true and complete Redemption which is related to "forty years," the closed Mem ם [which symbolizes the number forty] of "למרבה to the prosperity of the sovereignty and eternal peace."

(*Dvar Malchus* "*Concerning the advantage of the Jewish women and daughters, may they live, of our generation*" – *5752 (ch. 6)*)

Some Halachos and Instructions regarding Chinuch

Moshichai

Extra emphasis in educating children, who are referred to as Moshichai (Hashem's "anointed ones"), brings Moshiach. *(See Dvar Malchus Simchas Torah 5752 – Adaptation)*

The Mother's Role In Education

"We see that the education of boys and girls is mainly dependent on the Mother, especially Chinuch of small children and the smaller the child is the more it is dependent on the mother: she ingrains in them the liveliness and spirit of Yiddishkeit from when they are very small, and raised on this foundation are boys and girls occupied with Torah and its Mitzvos – in a pleasant and nice manner etc.

Meaning that in addition to bringing up the children to be fulfillers of Torah and Mitzvos on a simple level, the mother imbues in them the pleasure and warmth (with the gentleness and love which Jewish daughters and women naturally have) so that the fulfillment of the Torah and Mitzvos be in a good and nice way... As seen – for example – the good custom of Jewish mothers to sing to their very little children when they are still in their crib – that the Torah is the best thing, the sweetest thing, the nicest thing etc., which imbues in the child – also after he grows up – a deep love and value for all matters of Torah Mitzvos."

(Dvar Malchus "B'cha Yivarech Yisroel" – 22nd of Shvat 5752 (ch. 14) – Free Translation)

Permeated with Moshiach

The Rebbe King Moshiach Shlita says that children must be educated in a manner that the children become completely permeated through and through with the concept and point of "Moshiach," so that when one merely looks at a child they see "Moshiach." Their entire existence is "Moshiach" – expressed in perceiving that truthfully everything is Hashem. (See Dvar Malchus Simchas Torah 5752)

"...Among the main ways of saving the entire Jewish people is education of Jewish boys and girls – in the way of the Torah and Judaism, and ingraining in their hearts hope (and not losing hope,

Heaven forbid) for the Geulah through Moshiach Tzidkeinu very soon in our days. And then it 'turns over' 'that the Jews rule... and for the Jews   there was light, joy, gladness and honor.'..." (Igros Kodesh of the Rebbe King Moshiach Shlita (vol. 1, pg. 94) — Free Trans.)

Even when they grow up

Education of children should be in a manner that even when they grow up and are not under constant supervision they continue to act as they should. This is accomplished through revealing their Etzem HaNeshamah (the level of the essence of Moshiach – that Moshiach is physically alive among us). (See Dvar Malchus Vayechi 5752)

Obedience

In our times one should not scream at a child or hit a child; rather tell them what the Torah says they should do, explain to them why it is good for them to do so and show this to them by giving them candies and presents for their good conduct. (See Dvar Malchus Shoftim 5751, and more)

Kissing the Mezuzah etc.

Children kiss the Mezuzah a number of times during the day, especially when they wake up and before they go to sleep. It is important to educate children to say Bircas

Hamazon in a manner that they understand that they must thank Hashem for their physical food. (See Dvar Malchus Vayerah 5752)

Having their own Siddur etc.

We must make sure that every child has their own Siddur, Chumash etc., Tzedakah box and advisably their own small Tanya (in their room).

The abovementioned should be put in the children's room in a manner that they remind the child to use them (the Chumash etc. reminds the child to look at it, the Pushka reminds the child to put a coin in it) and likewise regarding all other aspects of children's Chinuch. (See Dvar Malchus B'cha Yivarech Yisroel" – 22nd of Shvat 5752, Bahalosecha 5751)

Both boys and girls should each have their own Sidddur and they should write in it, on the first page, "LaHashem HaAretz Umelo'ah" (The earth and everything in it belongs to Hashem) and below this write their Jewish name. (Being that everything should be connected to Moshiach it is a custom to write yechi also on the first page – See Dvar Malchus Eikev, 5751 – compiler).

(An excerpt of Likkutei Sichos vol. 14, pg. 279-80 – Adaptation)

Giving Tzedakah

In our generation we educate and accustom small Jewish children to give charity: in addition to giving them money to be given to charity, we also give them money for themselves, so that they should give from their own money to charity.

The children also have a part in building the third Beis Hamikdash through their donations for it, (as it was with regard to the contributions for the Mishkan). (See Dvar Malchus Terumah, 5752)

Kosher medicine etc.

It is important that children eat only Kosher food that an adult would eat. Even medicine or oral vaccines must be Kosher (a Rav should be consulted if this is not possible). Even a pregnant mother must be careful not to eat something unKosher even for medical purposes, and similarly when she is nursing. (See Igros Kodesh (vol. 1) of the Rebbe King Moshiach Shlita and more)

Toys etc. with Kosher animals

It is important for children to come into contact only with toys in the form of Kosher animals and not non-Kosher animals. Likewise when printing literature etc. we should use pictures of Kosher animals specifically. (See Sichos etc. of the Rebbe King Moshiach Shlita in the year 5744)

Children (and even grownups) should not have pictures in their room of non-Kosher animals birds or fish since they shouldn't see such pictures.

Pictures of non-Kosher animals to teach them that they aren't Kosher, or to describe an animal mentioned in the Torah is permitted.

Pictures of non-Kosher animals in a picture demonstrating a story of Torah in the Tenach or Midrashim of our Sages is permitted.

Seeing non-Kosher animals to contemplate upon the wonder of Hashem's creations is permitted – however only in a seldom manner; therefore going to the zoo is permitted.

Toys should be only of Kosher animals, birds or fish.
(Excerpts of Likkutei Sichos vol. 25, pg. 309 ff. – Adaptation)

- Being careful not to see non-Kosher animals is a timely matter, since we are preparing for the imminent coming of Moshiach, when Hashem will remove the spirit of impurity from the world, which includes removing the non-Kosher animals from the world.
  (Note, that we see a prelude of this today – we do not anymore ride on horses or transport with donkeys! – *the compiler.*)

(Excerpt of Likkutei Sichos vol. 25, ibid – Adaptation)

Importance of Chinuch

The general concept of Chinuch, since it is a necessary preparation for the fulfillment of the Mitzvos when the child grows up, it therefore gains importance and isn't a mere preparation rather an important matter itself, [and on the contrary: to a certain extent it is "higher" than the concept of an [actual] Mitzvah] and one must give himself completely over to it with all efforts and strength.

(Dvar Malchus Pinchas 5751 – Free Trans.)

Even Little Girls Light a Shabbos Candle

Even little girls should light a Shabbos (Yom Tov) candle (from when they are able to understand). They should light before their mothers so that their mothers can help them.

(Dvar Malchus "B'cha Yivarech Yisroel" – 22nd of Shevat 5752 (ch. 17) – Adapt.)

Through little girls lighting Shabbos candles (as well as other Mitzvos) and influencing their friends to do likewise we will very soon merit to see the Cohanim light the lamps of the Holy Menorah in the third Beis Hamikdosh, in the true and complete Redemption through Moshiach Tzidkeinu!

(An excerpt of Likkutei Sichos vol. 14, pg. 199 – Adaptation)

Tznius - From the Age of Three

According to Shulchan Aruch from the age of three and a day a girl must already conduct herself in a Tznius (modest) manner and most certainly a ten year old and older... however not to put great pressure ... and to speak in a pleasant manner.

(Likkutei Sichos vol. 18 pg. (448) – Free Trans.)

Little girls may come to Shul with their father (not only in the women's section) even after the age of three – until they reach the age of Chinuch in this matter (they understand the significance and content of separating the men from the women).

(An excerpt of Sefer HaSichos 5749, vol. 1, pg. 5 – Adaptation)

The Length of Dresses

....Regarding how long dresses should be it is known my opinion on this that the length which is equal for every person (Jewish daughters may they live) and in every place is that the knees should be covered even when sitting.

This is as mentioned, equal for everyone and the minimum.

However being that there are places that the above is not sufficient, being that in matters of Tznius and the like, in addition to the Tznius standards that may not be changed in every place, there are also details which are dependant on the custom of the place – with regard to being more stringent, but not to in being more lenient, as self understood – indeed it is incumbent upon every Rav and Moreh Hora'ah to investigate and give rulings regarding action.

It is important to add, that the necessity to be more stringent in accordance with the conditions of the place, does not necessarily mean that it is a mere stringency, for it is also possible that due to the conditions of the place – it is Asur Min Hatorah (a Biblical prohibition)...

(Likkutei Sichos vol. 18 pg. 447– Free Trans.)

Teaching Children on Shabbos

We should assemble gatherings of children (in addition to men and women) every Shabbos to get together in the synagogues and study-halls to teach them Torah etc. [e.g. make them a Farbrengen].

Chassidus and Mivtzoim

Also children should learn Chassidus and do Mivtzoim.

(See Dvar Malchus Va'era (ch. 11)) (See Dvar Malchus Korach 5751 – II, Likkutei Sichos vol. 17)

Jewish children have the privilege and reasonability to teach non-jewish children the Seven Noachide Laws (that they see in the street etc.), not through arguments with them rather, through being a good example of a religious Jew – through wearing a Yarmulka, making blessings before eating etc. When the non-Jewish child sees them doing so they will ask them what they are doing, the Jewish child will then explain at length to the non-Jewish child that Hashem creates the world etc.

(An excerpt of the address of the 20th of Menachem-Av, 5747 (unedited) – Adaptation)

The general fulfillment of Mitzvos before the Geulah Ha'amitis Vehashleimah is in a manner of Chinuch in comparison to the ultimate fulfillment of Mitzvos in the Geulah Ha'amitis Vehashleimah as it says in the Sifrei (Halachic Midrash) "although I exiled you from Eretz Yisroel you should be outstanding with Mitzvos, so that when you return it should not be something new to you." And through this we bring about the time when we fulfill the Mitzvos in the best way possible "as You truly desire," in the Geulah Ha'amitis Vehashleimah through Moshiach, literally immediately.

(See Likkutei Sichos Vayera 5751)

Following the Example of Rivkah Our Matriarch

• The fact that a girl – from the age she can understand – must light a Shabbos candle, in addition to her mother's lighting of Shabbos Candles, we see from our matriarch Rivkah. The Torah tells us that she lit Shabbos candles when she was only three years old even before she married Yitzchak, in addition to Avraham (and Yitzchak's) lighting of Shabbos Candles. (see Likkutei Sichos vol. 15, pg. 170)

• When a girl reaches the age of Bas Mitzvah she has the Mitzvah to light a Shabbos candle and recite the Berachah. Even a little girl before Bas Mitzvah needs to light due to the Mitzvah of Chinuch – since a father is obligated to educate his daughters to do Mitzvos – and therefore even a little girl recites the Berachah. With the Berachah she thanks Hashem for giving her the privilege to do this special Mitzvah. (Likkutei Sichos Vol. 9, in the beg. – adaptation)

• A little girl should light before her mother so that her mother can help her light.

• If for whatever reason the mother is not home for Shabbos, although a little girl lights with a Berachah this does not exempt the elders in the family from lighting Shabbos candles and therefore, the husband must light also with a Berachah. The reason for this is because she is not Bas Mitzvah yet and therefore cannot exempt someone who is Bar\Bas Mitzvah.

• It is important to make a Berachah before doing a Mitzvah and therefore the Mother should try to get her little daughter to recite the Berachah, and not only merely light. If the little girl can understand, it seems from the Sichos of the Rebbe Melech Hamoshiach Shlita, that although she cannot make a Berachah, nevertheless she should still light.

• All the above applies also to Yom Tov (Holiday) candles.

"The Zohar says that there is a deeper reason as to why specifically women are the ones who light the Shabbos candles – due to their great virtue they were given the honor of lighting Shabbos candles, Hashem chose them and gave them the merit and power

– To raise "holy children that will be the lamps for the world" through permeating their daily lives with "Mitzvah – a lamp, and Torah – light";

– To "bring much peace to the world" – including through Shalom Bayis (peace at home) which is enhanced by the Shabbos candles;

– To bring long life to her husband, herself, her children and grandchildren…

When a little girl lights Shabbos candles she brings in to the home Light and the dwelling of the Shechinah – Judaism and G-dliness…

This will hasten the coming of Moshiach when all the Jewish people joyously will go to the Holy Land, an eternal Redemption."

(Likkutei Sichos Vol. 9, in the beg. — adaptation)

True Nachas From our Children

Ahavas Yisroel

"Even if a person has something that another cannot get anywhere else in the world he has to be ready to give it up to help another Jew, even a Jew that may have sinned – in order to help him repent, and even if the action will not be called by his name. Moreover, he must consider this a merit that another Jew was helped by him, to the extent that he has true joy from this, and makes a family celebration, to celebrate.

In order to affect children to act in this manner we ourseleves must do our Service with self- sacrifice and complete submission to Hashem. Through this we raise a generation ready to give up – with joy – what they have to another Jew.

Great is the virtue of Ahavas Yisroel, love of a fellow Jew with no alterior reason, to bring the true complete Redemption, very soon."

(Likkutei Sichos vol. 4 – adaptation)

True Nachas

"Our Sages say the reward the Midwives in egypt received for giving life to the children is that Hashem made them "homes" of Kehunah, Leviah and Malchus (as we shall explain). Indeed, the greatest reward parents can have is raising children who establish Jewish homes. Sharp scholarly geniuses are nice but yet greater is helping Jewish people establish Jewish homes through influencing Jewish children to take part in Kehunah, Leviah and Malchus.

Kehunah – being separate from worldly negativity and uniting with G-dliness.

Leviah – being in the world and transforming it to Holliness. However this is not yet the ultimate since a Levi is still strongly connected to the Khanim, hence he can transform only things that still have some what of a connection to Holliness.

Malchus – the ultimate, bringing the kingship of Hashem throughout the entire world.

True Nachas of a Jewish mother is when she builds "homes" Jewish children that conduct themselves in a manner of in Kehunah, Leviah and Malchus, thereby all the Tzivos Hashem leave the final exile – just as the Tzivos Hashem left egypt that the Midwives established – lead by the king, with "a strong arm."

(Likkutei Sichos vol. 21, in the beg. – adaptation)

In its Literal Meaning

"Immidiatedly we shall have the fiest of the wild ox and leviathan, in the Time to Come, which as the conclusion in Chassidic teachings (based on the ruling of the Ramban) the main meaning of this is a physical meal in the literal sense. As a childs understanding of this – in its literal meaning."

[The Ramban rules that the ultimate state of the Time to Come is as the Jewish people are souls in bodies; likewise this meal is not (only) a spirtual phenomenon rather a literal physical meal.

Indeed children understand miraculous statements in the Torah to be literal in the physical sense – to them this is obvious without question! – compiler]

(Excerpt of an outline of the address of Vayikra 5751 – unedited)

The Greatness of Children

Tell children about their special greatness and power!

The following is just a tiny sample of the many places in which the Rebbe King Moshiach Shlita emphasizes the important role of Jewish children.

The Children Lead the Jewish People to Redemption

"...it was the children who first exclaimed, "This is my G-d!" For these were the children who in the very midst of the hardship and enslavement in Egypt were brought up in the true Jewish way.

"Inspired by such children, it was not difficult to...go out into the desert, without even any provisions, but with firm faith in the A-lmighty...

"Marching ahead with such children, Jews have no fear...the whole of Nature is transformed..." (Letters by the Lubavitcher Rebbe Shlita, vol. 1 pg. 263)

The Arizal says that the first generation of the ultimate Redemption is a reincarnation of the generation that left Egypt. The children of our generation, then, are those same children who led the Jewish People to redemption with their pure faith in Hashem.

Torah and Tzedakah of Children Bring the Redemption

In other letters the Rebbe King Moshiach Shlita calls on Jewish children to follow the example of the children in the time of Mordechai and Esther – who were the main ones who brought about the miracle of Purim – by adding in learning Torah and doing Mitzvos. This includes spending extra time learning Torah and also increasing the enthusiasm and concentration in learning, as well as to start or expand a free loan fund with their own pocket money. "...just as Jewish children helped bring about the deliverance of our people in the time of Mordechai and Esther, so now, too, Jewish children have it in their power – through Torah and Tzedoko – to help bring closer the True and Complete Geulo (deliverance) of our people through our Righteous Moshiach..."

(Letters by the Lubavitcher Rebbe Shlita, vol. 1 pg. 305-6 and 316-7)

An Army of Children

The Rebbe King Moshiach Shlita instituted "Tzivos Hashem" (the "Army of Hashem") – an army of Jewish children. His Majesty explains why the army is made up specifically of children, unlike when we went out of Egypt, when the army included only men of 20 years and older. When we left Egypt, it was necessary to fight a physical war using weapons, which necessitates adult strength. Regarding the ultimate Redemption, however, the verse says clearly that the Redemption will come in a calm and peaceful manner. Therefore, the army that brings the ultimate Redemption can even be of children. Moreover, it is especially through

children because they have a unique connection to Moshiach
– they are called "Meshichai".

(Likkutei Sichos vol. 28 pg. 236 ff.)

Belief in the Coming of Moshiach, Now!

"...Among the main ways of saving the entire Jewish people
is education of Jewish boys and girls – in the way of the
Torah and Judaism, and ingraining in their hearts hope (and
not losing hope, Heaven forbid) for the Geulah through
Moshiach Tzidkeinu very soon in our days. And then it
'turns over' 'that the Jews rule... and for the Jews there was
light, joy, gladness and honor.'..." (Igros Kodesh by Rebbe
King Moshiach Shlita (vol. 1, pg. 94) – Free Trans.)

The Correct Way to Teach the Alef-Beis

There is a traditional method that has been used throughout the generations, and the Rebbe King Moshiach Shlita strongly emphasizes the importance of using this method, known as "Komatz Alef Uh".

The children should be taught the names and shapes of the letters, then the names and shapes of the vowels. The names of the letters and vowels are holy and teaching them instills their holiness in the children. We should teach the children the *names* of the letters and vowels, not which sounds they make. Then we show the child an Alef with a Komatz under it, and say "Komatz Alef Uh", continuing to "Komatz Beis Buh" and so forth.

The Rebbe King Moshiach Shlita explains that the letters by themselves, as well as the vowels by themselves, do not have independent sounds. It is only when they are *combined* that they make a sound. (So we should not tell the children that Beis makes the Buh sound or that Komatz makes the Uh sound.)

According to the above, it would not be right to teach the Alef-Beis with pictures of what the letters stand for, or to show children words and tell them what the word says (sight-reading). We should teach the children in the traditional way, allowing the letters, vowels and their holy names to make their important impressions on the children.

It may be okay to teach older children – who already know how to read – concepts in the order of the Alef-Beis, but learning to read must be done in the traditional way because of its holy effect. The Rebbe King Moshiach Shlita says that we may teach the children the Alef-Beis using colorful letters.

This method of teaching the Alef-Beis has an important Moshiach lesson, which should be shared with the children and explained in a way that they can understand. As the Rebbe King Moshiach Shlita explains, the letters are "bodies" and the vowels are "Neshamos". Each alone has no independent sound, teaching us the importance of having *both* a body and a Neshamah. The ultimate unification of body and Neshamah is in the Redemption. Moshiach, who brings the Redemption and this ultimate unification, must also be a Neshamah *united* with a body – the Rebbe King Moshiach Shlita is always physically alive.

A way to connect the learning of the Alef-Beis (and any subject) to Moshiach is by saying Yechi before and after each learning session.

Thank you to Rabbi Goldstein for sharing his extensive research on this topic.

Education

Some Tips for Parents and Teachers

Through Torah study of children Jerusalem is rebuilt. As the Talmud states (Shabbos 119b) "Jerusalem was destroyed only as a result of them disturbing children from studying Torah," when the cause is nullified the result is nullified. This places greater emphasis on the fact that children are especially connected to the coming of Moshiach. *(Dvar Malchus, Simchas Torah 5752 – Adaptation)*

The three weeks is an opportune time to enhance the education of children, especially in making sure that the upcoming school year is a successful one. The following are excerpts from Sichos regarding education that will help us choose the right school and some tips for teachers and parents.

The Rebbe King Moshiach Shlita says:

"... Education of children must be in a manner that that the children become completely permeated, through and through, with the concept and point of "Moshiach," as such that when you merely glance at a Jewish child what do you see? Moshiach!..."

(Dvar Malchus, Simchas Torah 5752 – Free Translation)

When a teacher is "on the job" they must put their full attention on the children and not be occupied with anything else. Children especially can notice if someone is completely "with them" or is thinking about something else.

Even the Baal Shem Tov when he was a teacher's assistant (when he was a hidden Tzaddik) he was not occupied in "Lofty" matters during his assistance, rather his complete focus was on the children. *(Likkutei Sichos vol. 8, pg. 251 and more)*

Children should be taught also matters of Torah that transcend understanding (miracles etc.).

The Rebbe Rayatz related that when his children were young he took a teacher for them. They found out that the teacher was of the opinion that children do not have be told matters in Judaism that are astounding – miracles that are above understanding, wonders that are not logical... When they learned of his opinion, they immediately dismissed him.

(Likutei Sichos vol. 19 pg. 91 – *adaptation*)

A Jewish school is not only a place where a child receives information rather a place where children become servants of Hashem, this is accomplished through the teacher setting an example of good conduct. (*See also Dvar Malchus Pinchas 5751*)

In our times one should not scream at a child or hit a child; rather tell them what the Torah says they should do, explain to them why it is good for them to do so and show this to them by giving them candies and presents for their good conduct. (See Dvar Malchus Shoftim 5751, and more)

Secular studies should not be studied. *(See Likkutei Sichos vol. 16 pg. 251 ff.)*

This is especially related to our times: the era of Moshiach, for as the Rebbe King Moshiach Shlita says that in the Ultimate Redemption all sciences will be known from the Torah. Everything is found in the Torah – the greatest wisdom, and in the Ultimate Redemption this will be clearly revealed.

Even if secular studies are studied, it is important that they be pure and not immodest, no unKosher animals etc. (See Likkutei Sichos vol. 13 pg. 167)

The following is a free translation of Sichah of the Rebbe King Moshiach Shlita regarding preparations for the new school year and education.

"...We have already spoken many times recently (and I have requested to publicize this) concerning placing special efforts in the education of Jewish boys and girls Sheyichyu, and especially the education of little children, beginning with very little children. And especially in these days, being that the Seder in these countries is that the new school year begins in the month of Elul, behold this time must be utilized (and as the saying of our Sages "you go to a city, utilize its customs") for getting boys and girls to learn in kosher schools, and on a higher level – schools in which the education is with purity of holiness, to the extent of holy education, and then – as the saying of our Rebbeim – "as commences the onset that is how it continues, when one commences the onset straight it goes straight," and when the year will begin with kosher education and education with purity of holiness, behold the entire year will be in an upright and good manner.

Likewise effort should be placed to especially utilize these days in which the children are returning now from summer camps to their homes, and are preparing for the beginning of the new school year, indeed effort must be placed that immediately upon their return home and even before the beginning of their studies, that their education shall be with purity of holiness, and especially to put effort that these children (and all Jewish children) shall apply and be accepted to study in kosher schools, "purity of holiness" schools.

There is a special connection between the concept of education and the month of Elul:

In Likkutei Torah is explained the analogy (in connection with the month of Elul) that in these days Hashem is like a king who is found in the field and every person can (and must) come close to Him, and He shows a joyous countenance to every person, and receives them with a pleasant face.

Certainly this analogy is pertinent also to little children since they also are capable of understanding this analogy as long as it is explained to them, and for them there is a great and wondrous advantage when the King is found in the field (in comparison to as He is in His Royal Chamber) *even more* than for adults, since a child cannot enter to see the King when He is found in His Royal Chamber, whereas an adult – if he is a high official or the like – can enter. However when the King is found in the field indeed even a child can approach Him.

An additional difference is this between a child and an adult, that an adult has awe and fear of the King, which this can hold him back from approaching and accepting the King, whereas by a child his fear won't hold him back from coming close to something which is precious to him (as seen clearly that when he sees something precious and sparkling or the like, immediately he hastens to take it, as understood also the story with Moshe Rabbeinu). Only that he must be explained the greatness and value of the King, meaning, to educate him in a manner that the King should be precious in his eyes, and then automatically when the King will be in the field he will run towards Him etc.

And therefore especially these days should be utilized in order to add and draw more and more boys and girls to schools and Yeshivos which educate a kosher education and an education with purity of holiness.

And on a similar note in regard to adults, it is known that among the acronyms of the month of Elul is "Inah L'yadoi V'samti L'cha" representing the fact that the month of Elul is like a refuge city in which one sits peacefully since he has no fear of etc., and similarly in the month of Elul each and every person must add in Torah study and fulfillment of the Commandments along with peace from any disturbing matter and as a result – without any limits.

And through this we will merit to receive all the blessings, and especially, in the known wording "all of you shall stand prepared," to receive the blessing of Hashem to have an inscribing and sealing for a good and sweet year, obviously including the main blessing that it be a year of Redemption, the true and complete Redemption through Moshiach Tzidkenu.

(Likkutei Sichos vol. 14)

Some Instructions Regarding Family Purity

"...Children who will greet Moshiach very soon..."

In areas where as of yet there is no 'women and daughters Jewish outreach group' see to it to make one. The group should be occupied in spreading Judaism in general and for married women, spread the Mitzvah of family purity, with all its details.

Likewise those that are preparing for married life – they should have where to learn everything connected to family purity and learning it in the best and most complete way.

Including printing the laws and customs of this in the language of each country, as was done in many countries.

The booklets should printed with all the detailed laws including the highest level of their fulfillment, for just as people want their children to be born and grow up in the most perfect manner it is understood that the preparation for the birth as well as the preparation for the pregnancy, must be at the height of perfection.

These booklets should be distributed in a manner that it will be received by everyone who needs additional knowledge of these laws and customs.

Mainly there should be a women's group that will oversee all of this. Starting with being in contact with the Rabbi(s) that deal with the marriage ceremonies and find out who will be getting married in the near future,

And then find ways to know (in a pleasant and gentle manner) if there is a necessity for arousal and encouragement regarding family purity, so that the new home will be an eternal edifice built on the foundations of Torah and Mitzvos, and a house in which will be born healthy, radiant and religious children, who will greet Moshiach very soon together with their mothers and fathers, grandfathers and grand mothers.

There should be at least one such group in every city and if it is divided into towns in every town, and if there is different sects – in every sect, to guard the observance of family purity, moreover, they will encourage others regarding it.

Being that when things are merely told orally it is possible that the person will not absorb it well or forget and will be embarrassed to ask again – they should give along with this a booklet with the laws and customs.

The booklet should also have a list of all the locations of kosher Mikvahs in the entire city so that one will not be embarrassed to ask, and especially since some women like to go to a Mikvah that is close and some to one that is far.

(Adapted from the address of the 14th of Kislev, 5739)

Peace in the Home Through Family Purity

True unity between husband and wife is that they are both united in working for the same goal, namely, to serve Hashem. This is emphasized in keeping all the laws of family purity in all its details (being completely separate when they must etc.). Indeed, keeping the laws of family purity is an essential in having Shalom Bayis, peace in the home. Through this the husband and wife have children that hasten the Redemption through fulfillment of Torah and Mitzvos and will greet Moshiach, upon which the parents will proudly say "these are the children we have raised." *(Adapted excerpt of 19th Kislev 5739)*

Newlyweds

In addition to making sure the newlyweds have furniture it is important to make sure – first and foremost – that they have many Seforim (Jewish books) – a "house full of Seforim," including the meaning that the house be filled with the content of the Seforim.

As the custom in many places that they give a Shas as a present to the Chassan, and the the Kallah – a present a Siddur Korbon Minchah – today, however, it is better to give her instead Books of Jewish Law pertaining to taking care of the Home.

Obviously the more Seforim given as gifts, the better.

(Sefer Hasichos 5748, vol. 1, pg. 191 – *adaptation*)

A Beautiful
Home

According to the Instructions of the Rebbe King Moshiach Shlita

The ultimate dwelling for Hashem in the lowest realms as will be complete in the Geulah Ha'amitis Vehashleimah is mainly accomplished through Jewish women and girls. This is because they are the main ones who make Hashem a beautiful home both spiritually and physically.

(Dvar Malchus "B'cha Yivarech Yisroel" – 22nd of Shevat 5752 (ch. 11 -14) – adaptation)

A House Permeated with Moshiach

Women make a beautiful, vibrant, bright and fragrant dwelling place for Hashem below, including the ultimate perfection of "the light of Moshiach" and "the air of Moshiach"* in the Geulah, which comes in the merit of the righteous women!

*) See Dvar Malchus Toldos 5752 (2) ch. 11. [The revelation of Moshiach's existence

(liveliness) – as the King Moshiach is "the air of Moshiach." All the accomplishments of the Rebbe King Moshiach Shlita (revealing his majesty clearly to the whole world as Moshiach) and all the matters of the days of Moshiach, which we now see in the world are "the light of Moshiach." Indeed, the whole Redemption is an extension and outcome of Moshiach being here and alive with us just as a flame exists from the air around it. The announcement of "Long live our Master Teacher and Rebbe King Moshiach Forever" reveals the existence of the King Moshiach in the world.]

A House Full of Beautiful People and Children

Through Jewish women and girls keeping their three Mitzvos they make the "Home for Hashem" be a nice one, permeated with (spiritual and physical) beauty of Kashrus, purity and Holiness.

Eating Kosher changes the essence of the person because it becomes part of the person, and most certainly keeping Taharas Hamishpachah makes family life pure and nice along with good health physically and spiritually. Likewise Shabbos and Yom Tov candles bring Light and Holiness to the house and household. (Dvar Malchus "B'cha Yivarech Yisroel" – 22nd of Shevat 5752 (ch. 14) – adaptation)

Mezuzah and Women

"...Being that every Jewish women is the Akeres Habayis and every Jewish girl a future Akeres Habayis they have a special Zechus in the realm of Mezuzos, namely, not only to see to it to have a Kosher Mezuzah in one's own house on every door that needs a Mezuzah, rather also - by their neighbors, acquaintances and all Jewish houses..." (Likkutei Sichos vol. 14, pg. 204 - free trans.)

A House Full of Seforim

We should buy more and more Seforim to add to our "house full of Seforim." Likewise we should give other people presents of Seforim upon good occasions (birthdays etc.).

(Dvar Malchus Vayigash 5752 (ch. 13) – adaptation)

Kosher Seforim

We should make sure not to have any Seforim that have things in them that are opposite of the simple faith of the Jewish people (e.g. only the title Shlita and Melech HaMoshiach should be used for the Rebbe Melech HaMoshiach Shlita!).

(See Igros Kodesh of the Rebbe Melech HaMoshiach Shlita vol. 13 pg. 403 ff.)

Leaders of the House

"...Every man and woman is the "judge" and "advisor" of their house and household, and must lead the house according to the instructions and advice of the Torah..." (Dvar Malchus Shoftim 5751 ch. 12 - free trans.)

Pictures of the Rebbeim

Publicizing the Identity of Moshiach

In the Sichah of Shoftim 5751 the Rebbe King Moshiach Shlita asked to publicize to the entire generation that we have a Leader who is telling us the main prophecy that "here he (Moshiach) comes."

A few days after the Rebbe King Moshiach Shlita spoke these words (on the tenth of Elul) his Majesty said: now that we have said to publicize that "here he (Moshiach) comes" to the extent that you point with your finger and say this one (is coming), Moshiach is now revealed with the height of intensity.

Understanding their Teachings

Looking at the face of the Rabbeim, at the light of their faces, helps us understand their teachings. (Dvar Malchus Emor 5751 ch. 9)

Other Pictures

Kosher Animals

When printing literature etc. we should use pictures of Kosher animals specifically. (See Sichos etc. of the Rebbe King Moshiach Shlita in the year 5744)

The Menorah

Since the Menorah of the Mishkan and Mikdash had straight branches therefore pictures of the Menorah should be drawn with straight branches (not circular). This applies even to a Menorah in a logo which merely reminds a person of the

Menorah in the Mishkan and Mikdash. Also Chanukah Menorahs should have straight branches.

Immediately we should merit to see the Menorah in the third Beis Hamikdosh! (Likkutei Sichos vol. 21 pg. 169 - adap.)

Luchos

When drawing the Luchos they should be drawn square (not with two half circles on top rather as cubes) as the Luchos truly look. (Sefer Hama'amorim 5748, pg. 144 ff.- adap.)

A "Tzedakah House"

"...Most certainly everyone added in giving Tzedakah, including and especially - Tzedakah in a permanent manner, namely, that we make every house into a "house of Tzedakah" through building into the house a Tzedakah box, in a manner that it becomes a part of the building (according to Halachah), through which the entire house becomes "a house of Tzedakah"... through this the Tzedakah of Hashem is increased... including the ultimate Tzedakah for each and every Jew/Jewess among the Jewish people, and of all generations - that it should be a year of the Geulah Ha'amitis Vehashleimah through Moshiach Tzidkeinu swiftly in our days, Mamash..." (Sefer Hasichos 5749, at the beg. - free trans.)

A Kitchen "the Jewish Way"

The Geulah comes in the merit of righteous women. One of the reasons for this is because in the ultimate Geulah even the physical world will see G-dliness. The preparation for this is through making the physical things G-dly. This is especially done through women whose three Mitzvos deal with things that are necessary even for non-Jews - eating, light and family life and righteous women do all of these as the Torah prescribes.

(Likkutei Sichos vol. 20 pg. 218 - adap.)

The Place for the Shabbos Candles

At a public Seder in the year 5741 the Rebbe Melech Hamoshiach Shlita requested that they put the Yom Tov candles in a place that they can be seen while making Kiddush. The Rebbe Melech Hamoshiach Shlita explained: When you make Kiddush (on Shabbos or Yom Tov)" it is good to look at the candles" and it is understood that the phenomenon accomplished through this - reaches a high degree when he puts his eyes on the candles upon which the Berachah was made. Additionally: Shabbos and Yom Tov candles accomplish a number of things "so that we won't trip on things", when we eat the meal by the light of the candles we unite the two phenomena of "having pleasure on Shabbos"; and more. Therefore there should be by the meal (and not only by Kiddush) at least one of the candles upon which the Berachah was made.

(Hagadah Shel Pesach with Explanations etc. pg. 789 (in the 5747 print) - adap.)

Specific Practical Conclusions from the Above

We should fill our homes with Seforim.
Seforim should only have the titles "Melech HaMoshiach" and "Shlita" for the Rebbe King Moshiach Shlita.

We should have a picture of the Rebbe King Moshiach Shlita, with captions or wording publicizing that his Majesty is Moshiach. (For example, to have Yechi engraved on the frame.)

We should have pictures of only Kosher animals.

Menorahs and Luchos should be straight, not round.

We should build a Tzedakah box into the house.

We should eat and do all our physical activities according to Halacha.

The Shabbos candles should be in a place where the husband can look at them when he makes Kiddush, and where the Shabbos meal will be eaten.

The "Essence of the Home"

A woman, the "essence of the home" [and likewise her daughters that help her out and are preparing themselves to establish Jewish homes] accomplishes that the essence of the home be – Judaism, a house permeated with the light and warmth of Torah and Mitzvos, in a manner that this influences all those that dwell in the house – her husband, her children, that they all shall live lives of Torah and Mitzvos.

Including – through her accomplishing that all the parts of the physical home be vessels for spirituality, designated for Torah and Mitzvos, for example – through "a house full of Jewish books," and [having a] Tzedakah box and especially in the kitchen in which the food is prepared for the family – which this all adds in the success and blessing of Hashem in the food, and livelihood in abundance in general since there is the revelation and blessings from Hashem in the worldly maters.

Revealing Hashem even in worldly maters is especially emphasized when we see miracles – revealing G-dliness – in the world, especially in connection with the ultimate Redemption may it come immediately through Moshiach." (Excerpt from the 22nd of Elul, the Address to the Women, 5750 – adaptation)

The Virtue of Jewish Women!

The Rebbe King Moshiach Shlita often speaks about the great virtue of women and girls (mothers-to-be) that they have the power to affect the whole household, including the children and the husband in fulfilling Torah and Mitzvos – indeed every one of them is the "foundation of the home." The emphasizing of the virtue of women is related to the Geulah since in the Geulah the virtue of the Sefirah of Malchus (Hashem's 'Attribute' of Kingship) is revealed, and a woman corresponds to the Sefirah of Malchus.

The following is an interesting idea that came to mind (based on the words of the Rebbe King Moshaich Shlita, Tanya etc.) that will hopefully help us greater appreciate these ideas: one of the special achievements of the wife is making the house "a nice home" both physically and spiritually. This they do especially through lighting Shabbos candles, keeping the laws of family purity, keeping a kosher kitchen and being permeated with Moshiach, and spreading all this to others. In addition to all of this they make sure the house is neat and clean. A neat and clean house in the physical sense also adds to a good state of holiness in the home since "a nice home broadens one's mind," which helps us study Torah and keep Mitzvos in a better way.

Now if a woman has a lot of free time, it is easy for her to keep her house neat and clean and therefore this does not constitute such a major achievement. When is it an amazing achievement –when she has a very tight schedule. This is common for most Jewish women especially in our day of age; they Bli Ayin Harah have a lot of children, and put effort in doing Mitzvos and Mivtzoim etc. What gives a woman the power do the impossible of fulfilling Mitzvos in the best way, give good education to their children, do Mivtzoim and keep the house clean etc?

We may say the answer to this is based on their connection to the Sefirah of Malchus. The Sefirah of Malchus is referred to as "Ma'on" meaning: dwelling/house the source of this physical world. "Ma'on" is the same letters as "Noam" meaning pleasantness – the pleasantness of Hashem, the Essence of Hashem. "Ma'on" is the same letters as "Noam" because the source of Sefirah of Malchus is the Essence of Hashem. In the Geulah will be the ultimate revelation of the source of Sefirah of Malchus in the Sefirah of Malchus – the Essence of Hashem will be revealed in this physical world. Indeed, the Sefirah of Malchus also connects opposites. Only tha before the Geulah the part of Malchus that is revealed is the limitations of time and space – which make up the world. In the Geulah in the time and space itself will be revealed its source the Essence of Hashem that is above time and space.

The ability for the Sefirah of Malchus to unite opposites is due its Bittul (self nullification) to Hashem, which unites it with the infinite power of Hashem. In the Geulah this will reach its height.

As we approach the true and complete Geulah this is more and more revealed. This is possibly the explanation for the how the women are able to do the impossible. Through their Bittul they are able to bring into the limitations of the world the level that is above the limitations of the world, above time within time.

The one who emphasizes this and thereby gives the empowerment for this is the Rebbe Melech Hamoshiach Shlita who personifies the ultimate Bittul to Hashem. Indeed the seventh leader of Chabad corresponds to the seventh Sefirah the Sefirah of Malchus! Moshiach who brings the Geulah has the ultimate unification of the body (this limited physical world) and soul (a part of Hashem, above limitations) – as a soul in a body he receives the greatest revelations of Hashem.

It interesting to note that in the Likkutei Sichos of Chukas 5751 (the most recent as of yet for this Parshah) the Rebbe Melech Hamoshiach Shlita shows us clearly that he knows the future and tells us what is truly happening – on the Sunday of Parshas Chukas (5754 – the 3rd of Tammuz) we are to be certain that the Rebbe Melech Hamoshiach Shlita is alive as a soul in body and did not pass away, heaven forbid. In that Sichah the Rebbe Melech Hamoshiach Shlita explains a verse in the Chumash of the Sunday of Parshas Chukas at great length regarding "Tzamid Psil" – a seal on vessel that keeps everything inside it pure from the impurity of the opposite of life.

The Sichah discusses the way to be safe from impurity, the opposite of life, which is a result of the world having a negative influence on the person. The soul itself cannot not be influenced by the world only after it comes into a body (a vessel) it receives connection to the world and

may be influenced by it, Heaven forbid. One way to avoid this is through revealing the soul to such a great extent that it overwhelms the limitations of the body, and the second way is to refine the body to a very great extent – in both cases the body does not conceal over the Neshamah. These two ways however are each slightly imperfect since they both have relation to negativity (as explained at length in the Sichah). The Sichah concludes that if a person is in the attic where the impurity of the 'opposite of life' is not present (the impurity is in the lower floor) then he is impure – the way to avoid impurity is not through leaving this world rather through being in it and working with it.

Now in the middle of the Sichah in footnote 28 (Yechi) the Rebbe Melech Hamoshiach Shlita says that the two abovementioned ways were personified by Moshe and Eliyahu. And then (with seemingly no connection to the Sichah that only discusses two ways) the Rebbe Melech Hamoshiach Shlita adds an additional paragraph and writes "And see the Discourses of the Mitler Rebbe, Derushei Chasunah, vol. 1 pg. 131: the special level and advantage that Moshiach has even over Chanoch, for Chanoch had to unclothe from bodily physicality when he ascended to Heaven [he did not pass away, rather ascended to heaven alive – however, his body ceased to be physical], whereas Moshiach will remain in his body with the his high sourced Soul, in this physical world, just as he is sourced Above literally (and it is understood from there that he is also higher than the body of Eliyahu). Study [what is written] there (and ibid pg. 138 ff.) at length."

Indeed Moshiach personifies the ultimate Service of Hashem IN TORAH AND MITZVOS AND THERFORE DOES NOT PASS AWAY! This is the fact, and the women, especially, are certain of this fact and do all they can – including having a good influence on their family – so that we will all open our eyes and see this fact: the Rebbe Melech Hamoshiach Shlita in his full glory, Now!

Some Important Instructions for Women

From the Words of the Rebbe King Moshiach Shlita

✍The daily study of Rambam is also for women. Either three chapters a day or if they are not able to do three they may do one chapter a day or the daily portion of Sefer Hamitvos of the Rambam. Emphasis should be placed especially on studying the last two chapters of Rambam (in his 14th book "Shoftim") – "the laws of Moshiach."

✍ Women are obligated to study the laws of the Mitzvos that they must fulfill. They are also obligated to study Chassidic teachings, since the fulfillment of the fundamental Commandments, which are a constant obligation (and therefore are an obligation for women as well), namely, the belief in Hashem and His oneness, loving and fearing Him etc., are dependent on the study of Chassidic teachings. They should also study topics of Moshiach and Redemption.

✍ Women gain merit by bringing their children to the synagogue… and waiting for their husbands [to come home from the study- hall.]

✍ Women are obligated in the Mitzvah of Mezuzah and being that they are "the foundation of the home" they have a special connection to this Mitzvah – they should make sure the state of Mezuzos in their house as well as in others houses is as it should. Moreover, for women the Mitzvah of Mezuzah has precedence over other Mitzvos since their life is dependent on it (e.g. when influencing other women to do Mitzvos among the first Mitzvos we should have influence upon them is the Mitzvah of Mezuzah – the compiler).

🖙Women are obligated in all Negative Mitzvos (not
desecrating the Shabbos etc.) and all Positive Mitzvos that
are not time bound (giving charity etc.). Women are exempt
from doing most Positive (active) Mitzvos that are time bound
e.g. Tefillin, Tzitzis etc.; excluding the Mitzvah of Matzah,
Shabbos candles, praying Shacharis (in the morning) and
Minchah (in the afternoon), remembering the exodus of
Egypt in the morning and at night1 and more which they are
obligated to fulfill. The Arizal explains the reason they are
exempt from those Mitzvos: since a man and wife are each
the half of one body – when the husband (or future husband)
fulfills them it exempts the wife who is his second half from
fulfilling them.2

🖙 Women make a blessing over all Positive Mitzvos that are
time bound even those that they are exempt from fulfilling
them. Therefore, women make a blessing over shaking Lulav
eating in the Sukkah etc.

🖙 We must be careful be careful the customs of Jewish
education for children, notwithstanding the fact that the
children don't understand or give much attention to
what they see or hear. E.g. when teaching children how
to read Hebrew they must be taught the vowels – as
follows "Kametz Alef Uh" and so forth (and not merely
show them the vowel and say this makes an "Uh" sound
and show it to them under the Alef and tell them this is
read "Uh").

We must even be careful to keep the customs of
educating very small children, infants. (E.g. making
sure even little baby boys wear Yechi Yarmulkas (or

Yechi baby hats), making sure even little infants wash Negel Vasser – the compiler).

Jewish customs are very important and should be kept with the same amount (or even more) accuracy and carefulness as actual Mitzvos.

✍ Women today (who have their own money) may give large donations to charity.

✍ The advantage of a Shaitel over a Tichel is that a Shaitel guarantees the covering of all of the woman's hair all the time, as required by the Shulchan Aruch. Wearing a hat or even a Tichel, leaves part of the hair uncovered at least for a short time thereby transgressing the ruling in Shulchan Aruch that all the hair must be covered all the time. Whereas when a woman covers all her hair with a Shaitel it brings much blessing upon them and their family.3

Wearing a Shaitel also eliminates the possibility of a woman suddenly uncovering part or all of her hair.4

✍ Women and girls have a good Jewish custom to give coins to charity prior to the lighting of Shabbos candles.

1 Truthfully, this is not considered a time bound Mitzvah, rather a Mitzvah to constantly remember the exodus from Egypt.

2 This paragraph is based on the Shulchan Aruch of the Alter Rebbe and the words of the Rebbe Melech Hamoshiach Shlita.

3 See Igros Kodesh of the Rebbe King Moshiach Shlita vol. 19, pg. 488, see there at length.

4 See Igros Kodesh of the Rebbe King Moshiach Shlita, vol. 10 pg. 186, and more.

Instructions of the Rebbe King Moshiach Shlita Regarding

Tznius-Modesty

Tznius, modesty, is a great virtue – "the true honor of the king's daughter is her modesty". The mothers of the Jewish people: Sarah, Rivkah, Rachel and Leah, conducted themselves in a modest manner – indeed, Tznius is the foundation upon which every Jewish house stands.

The reward is also great: through the conduct of the Jewish righteous women in this manner, we merit that the Land of Israel is peacefully quiet including the ultimate perfection of this in the true and complete Redemption!

(Excerpt from Dvar Malchus Bo-Beshalach 5752 – adaptation)

All Aspects of Tznius

Tznius is not only regarding how one dresses but also – that girls and women should sing and dance only in the presence of other women and girls.

Tznius also includes be careful with the laws of Yichud – to be careful not to be in a secluded area with a man that is not one's husband.

(See Dvar Malchus Bo-Beshalach 5752)

Tznius Even At Home

It is important that girls and women dress and act in a Tznius manner even in their own house and even when they are the only one home. The Talmud relates that Kimchus said that the walls of her house never saw her hair. In this merit, she had seven sons that merited being Kohanim Gedolim (high priests).

It is important to be Tznius even at home since this will help to be Tznius even when others are present at home etc., so that they won't forget etc.

Indeed, utmost modesty and good conduct of the parents even when the children are very little has an affect on them even when they grow up.

(Excerpt from an address on the 18th of Elul, 5742 – adaptation)

Tznius – The Times of Moshiach

It is important for all women to cover their entire hair and to be Tznius in the home since we are now in the time of the

Redemption. In the Redemption through Moshiach the walls will bear testimony to everything that is going on in the house. Indeed in the Redemption the walls will express G-dliness and Tznius conduct.

(see Likutei Sichos vol. 4)

Tznius Brings the Redemption

In the merit of the Jewish people – especially the Jewish women and girls – not changing their Jewish modest clothes to non- Jewish clothes we were redeemed from Egypt.

Similarly, regarding the ultimate Redemption – it comes in the merit of the Jewish people not changing their clothes to non–Jewish clothes.

(Likkutei Sichos vol. 8)

Wearing A Shaitel

Wearing a Sheitel is an essential for the good of one's children and grandchildren, livelihood and health as stated in the Zohar (vol. 3, 126a)...

[This Zohar speaks about the importance of a woman covering all of her hair (not even one hair uncovered) even in the house – compiler]

...In aforetimes, women would shave their heads to make sure their hair was completely covered. Now since they do not do this, the only way to cover all the hair is only possible when wearing a Sheitel...

Three Jewish women revived the entire Jewish community of Frankfurt and made it into a very religious place through being persistent to wear Sheitels, keep family purity and good education for their children, although in the beginning the reformed were strong there.

(Excerpts from Likkutei Sichos vol. 13 pg. 188 ff. – adaptation)

Sheitel: Head-Covering of the Redemption

Wearing a Shaitel Is Intrinsically Connected to Moshiach and Redemption

The Deeper Reason Why a Woman Must Cover Her Hair / The Relation of a Shaitel Specifically to Our Times: The Days of Moshiach - the Rebbe Shlita / A Story Expressing This Idea

The following is a deeper reason – based on the words[3] of the Rebbe King Moshiach Shlita – for why the Torah obligates Jewish women to cover their hair.

A woman represents Hashem's aspect of Malchus. Malchus of Atzilus is an Aspect of Hashem that is an extremely great Revelation, which transcends vestment in Vessels (Vessels contain the Light and draw it down to be revealed in the lower worlds). Since it is such a great revelation, it must have:

1) An extreme contraction so that it can transfer G-dly Light to the lower worlds. This contraction is referred to as hairs, since hair has a small amount of life in it. These "hairs" contract the Revelation to the extent that through them G-dly Sustenance is given to mundane matters as well, so that they may also continue to exist thereby giving us the opportunity to make a dwelling for Hashem in the lowest realms (whereas Greater G-dly Revelations would completely "blow away" mundane matters). However this alone is not sufficient since contraction and concealment on its own is negative – *concealment of G-dliness*.

Therefore there also must be: 2) The Revelation of Light *in the proper vessels* so that this great Revelation should be revealed below, and that the world may run in the correct manner. This makes the contraction not be negative rather it is for the purpose of revelation. Through the G-dly Light being vested in vessels it is distributed correctly, transferred in the correct fashion so that the mundane matters get their exact portion of G-dly Sustenance.

[A possible parable for this may be: Even if water is poured from the spout of a pitcher (step 1 – contracting it

---

[3] *See Likkutei Sichos vol. 23 pg. 348 and the references that are cited there. See also Dvar Malchus Tazria - Metzora 5751.*

(instead of the whole bottle pouring out in an instant)), it is still useless and counterproductive if there is no cup to receive it therefore it needs step 2 - (vested in a vessel)].

A woman's hair must therefore be covered (vested in a vessel).

The reason why a woman must wear a Shaitel and not a Tichel is because a Shaitel guarantees the covering of all of the woman's hair all the time, as required by the Shulchan Aruch,[4] and eliminates the possibility of her suddenly uncovering part or all of her hair.[5]

We may possibly explain the deeper reason behind the advantage of a Shaitel over a Tichel based on the explanation of the abovementioned concepts in our Avodas Hashem, as follows:[6]

The transcendent aspect of the Revelation of Malchus – represented by a woman's hair – is characteristic of Rotzoi. Rotzoi is contemplating upon the Greatness of Hashem to the extent that one wants to leave his body in order to cleave to Hashem, thereby not being revealed below. This must however be followed by Shuv – realizing that Hashem wants G-dliness to be drawn into this world and acting accordingly in learning Torah and fulfilling Miztvos with physical objects – which makes the Revelations of Hashem be distributed

---

[4] *See Igros Kodesh of the Rebbe King Moshiach Shlita vol. 19, pg. 488 "...wearing a hat or even a Tichel, leaves part of the hair uncovered at least for a short time..." See there that this transgresses the ruling in Shulchan Aruch, whereas when one covers all their hair with a Shaitel it brings much blessing upon them and their family – see there at length.*

[5] *See Igros Kodesh of the Rebbe King Moshiach Shlita, vol. 10 pg. 186, and more.*

[6] *See the sources cited in note 2.*

correctly in the proper vessels and are revealed in this world. Indeed, the world of Tikkun (Shuv) – drawing G-dliness below, comes after the world of Tohu (Rotzoi).

However, the ultimate Avodas Hashem is when the Rotzoi and Shuv are united as one, namely that in the Shuv itself the Rotzoi is clearly evident.[7] Meaning that the world itself expresses G-dliness; the lights of Tohu (Rotzoi) are in (and expressed through) the vessels of Tikkun (Shuv). This is also expressed in our generation in connection with the imminent true and complete Geulah (when this will reach perfection) in the fact that the body (Shuv) is intrinsically connected to the soul (Rotzoi) and we will not pass away or be buried, especially the Rebbe King Moshiach Shlita.[8]

Similarly, a Tichel is the Shuv (vestment in a vessel) however, after (i.e. clearly different than) the Rotzoi (hair), whereas a Shaitel is that in the Shuv itself (the vestment in a vessel), the Rotzoi is clearly evident (it looks like her own hair).

Before I wrote this article, I remembered a story expressing this idea. A friend of mine was wearing a Yechi Yarmulka when he was attending a Yeshivah who had students who bothered him about his Yarmulka. By Hashgachah Pratis he came across volume 15 of Igros Kodesh (page 198) where the Rebbe Melech Hamoshiach Shlita writes as follows "...it is simply understood that there must be an absolute condition which cannot be otherwise regarding a Sheitel... and this is not only a personal matter; rather also a public matter and meriting the public... even if

---

[7] *See Dvar Malchus Bamidbar 5751. See also Dvar Malchus Tazria-Metzora 5751, ch. 8.*

[8] *See Dvar Malchus Tazria-Metzora 5751, ch. 8, and Dvar Malchus Bo 5752, ch. 13.*

she will say that regarding her there is no difference in what manner she covers her head since it will be covered correctly in any case … it is possible that he will object regarding the custom of the Imahos that it wasn't specifically with a Sheitel… indeed this is one of the blessings of the era of Moshiach that 'a daughter shows brazenness to her mother' etc. and etc. in adding in observance of the Torah and Mitzvos…" Indeed, just as a Yechi Yarmulkah expresses that Moshiach is alive – the message of the time, similarly does a Shaitel for a woman[9]!

---

[9] *A Shaitel expresses the unification of Rotzoi and Shuv – soul and body – in the Geulah, epitomized by Moshiach.*

The importance of wearing a Sheitel

In a letter, the Rebbe King Moshiach Shlita praises a woman for happily resolving to wear a Sheitel, especially because she was one of the first ones in her community to "bring back this custom of the proper Jewish daughters", and others will follow her example. His Majesty offers to lend her money from a special fund for such things so that she can buy a Sheitel immediately, and urges her to let his Majesty know who to write the check to immediately upon receiving the letter. (Igros Kodesh vol. 8 pg. 192)

*

In response to the notification that a woman has begun to wear a Sheitel, the Rebbe King Moshiach Shlita blesses her that all Hashem's promises of rewards for women covering their hair completely should be fulfilled. His Majesty wrote this letter between Purim and Pesach, and mentions that at those times the women brought about miracles. The Rebbe King Moshiach Shlita goes on to wish her and her husband a Kosher and happy Pesach, and the speedy fulfillment of their desire to have children. (Igros Kodesh vol. 8 pg. 304)

The Rebbe King Moshiach Shlita says that we should make all physical objects "shine on their own" with holy light, in a way that we do not have to constantly do something to make sure that they are holy, and in fact they themselves should remind us to do Mitzvos. (See Dvar Malchus Beha'aloscha 5751 (1991).) A Sheitel "shines on its own" because it always covers the hair completely, without constantly having to be checked and fixed. This is unlike a kerchief, which often slides back and reveals hair. (See Igros Kodesh)

Modest Dress

Compiled by Ilanna Benyaminson

Hashem gave women a unique, special privilege and responsibility: dressing modestly. It makes us respectable and self-respecting. It is beauty of a high quality. It helps us look at our bodies in a positive, healthy way, and helps us express our real, higher selves. In the Redemption, the fact that we are the children of Hashem, the King of Kings, will be clearly revealed. Let us prepare for that by dressing like who we really are: holy princesses.

The following are some practical conclusions compiled from a Yechidus (private audience) of the Rebbe King Moshiach Shlita with Rabbi Shneur Zalman Gafne, at which his Majesty emphasized that women should help each other improve the modesty of their clothing.

- Women should gather together and discuss how to improve the modesty of their clothing. It is important for women themselves to discuss this with each other – when it comes from the women themselves it is much more effective than when someone outside forces it on them. Women should speak to other women about modest clothing, in a way of "words that come from the heart enter the heart".

- Skirts should be long but should not reach the ground, because this can be counterproductive to the goal of modesty. The longer the skirt, the better (yet not reaching the floor). The exact length should be decided by the rabbis who make Halachic rulings (Rabbonim). The minimum length is ten centimeters below the knees, so that the knees will be completely covered while sitting. This is the bare minimum, and it is praiseworthy to wear a skirt longer than this.
- Women should not wear tight-fitting clothing.
- It is not necessary to wear short skirts or skirts that reach the floor, or tight clothing, in order to look nice. Women should dress nicely, and according to the rules of modesty.
  Let us dress in a way befitting the true and complete Redemption, when we will all fulfill Hashem's will in the most perfect way. This will prepare us for and hasten the time when everyone will see the Rebbe King Moshiach Shlita – immediately NOW, Amen!

Clothing

It is especially important for teachers – both of higher grades and young children– to be careful about dressing in a way that befits a Jewish woman. This includes not only following the laws of modesty but also dressing in a Jewish way rather than according to non- Jewish fashions. One of the main reasons that the Jewish People were redeemed from Egypt was that they did not change their style of clothing to conform to Egyptian fashions.

(See Igros Kodesh vol. 9, pg. 216 and more.)

Once a mother brought her three- year-old daughter to visit Rebbetzin Chaya Mushka. It was hot, and the girl took off her jacket, revealing a sleeveless dress. The Rebbetzin told the mother that she should make sure that her daughter wears modest clothing – long sleeves – from now on, because from the age of three a girl must dress according to the laws of modesty. She said that modest clothing reflects a modest personality, and that a girl's dress reflects on her parents.

*

There is a famous story of a little girl who came to receive a dollar from the Rebbe King Moshiach Shlita. His Majesty told her that if she would dress modestly the next time she came, she would get two dollars. After much time, the girl had finally learned how to dress modestly and obtained the right clothing. She came again to receive a dollar from the Rebbe King Moshiach Shlita. The line was moving fast and after receiving one dollar she was pushed ahead. But then the Rebbe King Moshiach Shlita called her back and gave her a second dollar. His Majesty remembered her even though hundreds of people had come by to receive dollars since she had first come.

A Way to Get Your Daughter Excited About Tznius

When your daughter plays with dolls, encourage her to dress them in Tznius clothes. This can be a fun way to teach her the laws of Tznius. The Rebbe King Moshiach Shlita says that when girls play with dolls, they are preparing for their future role as mothers (see Likkutei Sichos vol. 14).

Royalty

Modest clothing is a sign of dignity and self- respect, befitting Jewish women and girls, who are daughters of Hashem, the King of Kings. By dressing modestly, we prepare for and begin to taste the time when this royalty of the Jewish People will be fully revealed – in the true and complete Redemption.

Tznius and the Time to Come

Among the blessings Asher received were: 1– he was blessed with abundance of oil "he will immerse his foot in oil," 2– the blessing of having a bountiful year in the year ushering the Shemmitah year – so they would have food during the Shemmitah year – was given to Asher and the other tribes would receive their sustenance from his tribe, 3– his daughters married Cohenim Gedolim. What do these three blessings have in common?

"He will immerse his foot in oil," alludes to the virtue of Kabbolas Ol (acceptance of the Yoke of Heaven) complete submission to Hashem even if we don't understand, similar to the foot which has a virtue over the head. Intellect is compared to oil and therefore "He will immerse his foot in oil" means that the oil is secondary to the foot – even the understanding must be preceded by and based on Kabbolas Ol: because "so said Hashem."

Shemmitah is a Mitzvah that is connected to physicality, physical food, moreover one can even have a question "what will we eat," in such a case we need Kabbolas Ol. Through Kabbolas Ol to fulfill this Mitzvah Hashem gives His Blessing.

His daughters married Cohenim Gedolim because they were beautiful. The true beauty of a Jewish women is her Tznius (modesty) – "the honor of a King's daughter is her modesty." [This also is Kabbolas Ol in a physical matter – through being spiritually beautiful – Tznius, Hashem helps them have this in the simple sense.]

Through the service of in accordance with the Shulchan Aruch (Code of Jewish Law) including women's Tznius we merit the Time to Come when, the virtue of action will be revealed – at that time we will truly appreciate the virtue of accomplishing a lot, being careful with every detail of Jewish law more than the quality of being smart. *(Likkutei Sichos vol. 1, pg. 102 ff. - adaptation)*

Makeup

Makeup is used to bring out a woman's natural beauty so that she will look beautiful for her husband. This is especially important in the first thirty days of marriage, when the wife is called a "Kallah" (bride), as is expressed in certain Halachos. Hashem and the Jewish People are compared to a husband and wife. The Giving of the Torah is the "wedding", and this event repeats itself every day, as we say every day that Hashem gives the Torah, in present tense. This means that we are always Hashem's Kallah and constantly need "makeup" to bring out our inner beauty. Just as all Jewish daughters are beautiful, but poverty can hide their beauty, so too the Jewish People are beautiful but their spiritual "poverty in knowledge" sometimes hides this, also causing literal physical poverty. Hashem, in His great mercy, gives us Tzaddikim who perform miracles, revealing G-dliness and thereby helping us to leave our limitations and serve Hashem in a beautiful manner. Though makeup is external, it is important to use it in order to bring out our inner beauty for our husbands. We can learn from this how important it is to express our inner Jewish feelings in actual performance of Torah and Mitzvos, including dressing modestly.

The Women's Section

One of the main parts of the Beis Hamikdosh is the Ezras Nashim (literally 'the women's section'). In the Ezras Nashim there were balconies for the women. It is stated in the Gemarah Sukkah (51b ff.) that originally the men were outside and the women were inside – yes the women enter the Beis Hamikdosh. The Sages later instituted the balconies so that the men would be below and the women above in order to guarantee Tznius (modest) behavior.

The Rebbe Melech Hamoshiach Shlita mentions that we see from here that women and girls may gather in the men's section of the Shul – not during the time of prayer of course (since there is no Mechitzah and men are present then). This is the basis for the custom of the Rebbes to speak to women and girls when they are gathered in the men's section of the Shul of the Shul when the men are not there.

Balconies for the Women

The Rebbe Melech Hamoshiach Shlita writes that the above-mentioned balcony for women in the Beis Hamikdosh is one of the sources for the necessity to have a Mechitzah in Shul, and that the Mechitzah must prevent the men from seeing the women – which for this reason the women were on top and the men on the bottom. If in the Beis Hamikdosh in which the awe of Hashem fell upon everyone, nevertheless it was necessary to have a Mechitzah, a Shul which is a miniature Mikdash certainly needs a Mechitzah. When we do this the Shul becomes a House of Prayer for Hashem, where the prayers of the Jewish people are accepted.

Mechitzah

Partition between Men and Women

The Reason for a Mechitzah

The division of a Mechitzah brings true peace and unity. The reason for this is because two opposites cannot truly combine for combining them causes one of them to be nullified (e.g. fire and water). Specifically when they are separate and do their unique job in serving Hashem are they truly united "united in serving One Creator" as will reach ultimate perfection in the True and Complete Redemption through Moshiach – who brings the ultimate peace.

(Adapted from Likkutei Sichos vol. 18 pg. 210 ff.)

Here are some interesting points quoted (free translation) from the above mentioned talk of the Lubavitcher Rebbe King Moshiach Shlita explaining the importance of separating between men and women, which will give a better understanding of this issue:

"There are those who claim that for the sake of peace and Kiruv Halevavot we must not be strict about the Mechitzot and separations that Hashem set up in the world - starting from taking away the Mechitzah and separation between men and women...including them in a Minyan etc.; trying to make a mixture in religion and Emunah between Jews and Lehavdil the nations of the world; a break in the separation between the Jewish People and the nations, Heaven forbid, through so-called 'conversion' not according to Halachah...

"When we want, Heaven forbid, to nullify the boundaries that 'Hashem put *in His world*', then in addition to the main thing - that this is the opposite of the Torah of Moshe, which is the Torah of Hashem...we do not bring any peace, rather, the opposite: Pirud Halevavot,

"Things that are essentially separate or are opposites of each other, cannot have any connection between them, unless it is through a Mechitzah that separates between them [for example, the connection of 'water' and 'fire' can exist specifically when there is a separation (of the pot in which the water is, etc.). Otherwise, there is no purpose to the connection; rather, the connection brings a complete nullification of the existence of both].

"Specifically through upholding and strengthening the Mechitzot and boundaries that Hashem created, peace is accomplished, which is necessary between different types, because it is a peace that is built on Torah, that 'all her pathways are peace';

"And through this we merit the time when 'there will be no...war and no jealousy and competition', Moshiach comes, who is a descendant of David and Shlomo (and about Shlomo it says 'he will be a man of Menuchah...and peace and quiet I will give upon the Jewish People in his days') - although then also the Jews will be separate from the nations of the world as it says 'and foreign people will stand...' - 'and he will correct the entire world to serve Hashem together as it says 'for then I will transform the nations to have a clear speech for all of them to call out in the Name of Hashem and to serve Him only'." (Likkutei Sichot vol. 18, pg. 210-211)

Mechitzah at a Wedding

If one truly wants the Torah to rule that a wedding be a joyous one – at the wedding shall be said "blessed are You, our G-d *which the joy is in His abode...*" and through this afterwards the newly weds will be happy their entire life, Shulchan Aruch says *that a the wedding there must be a Mechitzah.*

(Likutei Sichos vol. 9, pg. 332 ff. – adaptation)

It is important to note that the source the Rebbe King Moshiach Shlita cites for the law that there must be a Mechitzah at a wedding says that when men and women are together without a Mechitzah the evil inclination is present and therefore Hashem is not at Joy, hence "blessed are You, our G-d *which the joy is in His abode...*" is not recited. Hence also at a Sheva Berachos when we also recite "blessed are You, our G-d *which the joy is in His abode...*" a Mechitzah is necessary.

Why Gender Separation is Good for Women

By Ilanna Benyaminson

The Rebbe King Moshiach Shlita says that because men and women are compared to water and fire, it is important for them to be separated so that they can each exist; when water and fire are mixed, either the water extinguishes the fire, or the fire causes the water to evaporate. Studies today have shown that *separate schools* for boys and girls cause the students to learn better, whereas in coed schools the girls do not participate enough and the boys are too overpowering. When the genders are separated, each can shine.

When the genders are separated, women can be more active, form friendships and focus on the things that interest us and that we are good at. The stronger the separation, the more the women can shine.

Some examples:

Separate Farbrengens. Rather than women listening passively to a men's Farbrengen, women can have their own Farbrengens, where they discuss topics that specifically interest women – education of children, dressing modestly, the wife's role in improving a marriage, moving personal stories, etc. They can also sing, which they cannot do while at a men's Farbrengen. And they can prepare special foods and decorations that women are good at making and appreciate. They can open up, share their stories, experiences and challenges, and strengthen each other.

Simchas Beis Hashoevah. Instead of watching men dance, which can be very boring, women can have separate Simchas Beis Hashoevah celebrations by renting a hall etc. They can hire female dance instructors, musicians and singers, bring tambourines and actively rejoice!

Simchas Torah. Women can dance separately from the men instead of passively watching them. Women express their joy differently than men do. Women can go into a different room where the men cannot hear them singing, to a different building or to someone's home for a feminine-style dancing celebration. They can bring a dance instructor to make it interesting, and some talented female singers to lead the singing.

Although women enjoy seeing the Sifrei Torah, this is not a reason to take away the Mechitzah, which can often lead to inappropriate mingling. Even a half-Mechitzah can cause women to feel uncomfortable and can distract the men from their concentration on the Hakafos, which are actually a part of Davenning (they are a series of requests from Hashem). Most women do not actually watch the Hakafos the entire time, and can get bored or end up just schmoozing. It is much more fun and meaningful for women to dance themselves.

There is a story about Chassidim doing Hakafos with a Tanya. Perhaps women can dance with Tanyas.

Davenning. It is universally accepted in Orthodox Shuls that a Mechitzah is needed for Davenning so that the men should not be distracted from their concentration. For the women, it enables them to Daven with feminine emotion, with the moral support of the other women around them. It also becomes a place for them to meet friends and get to know each other (after Davenning, of course), strengthening the unity of the community. If men and women would be mixed, many women would be likely to stick with their husbands rather than reaching out and meeting other women.

There is an interesting letter by the Rebbe King Moshiach Shlita in which his Majesty writes that if it is impossible to have a Mechitzah in a Shul, they should either have a separate Shul for the women or have the men and women Daven at separate times. Maybe it would be an idea to organize women's prayer groups. Even though it would not be considered a Minyan and certain parts of the service would be omitted, women (who have no obligation to Daven with a Minyan anyway) could focus on their special feminine Davenning talent; after all, we learn the Halachos of Shmoneh Esrei from Chanah's prayer. On Friday night, there are not so many differences between the Davenning in a Minyan and Davenning without a Minyan. In many girls' camps and seminaries, this is a special time for the girls to sing almost all of the Davenning together and to dance after Lechah Dodi. At most Shuls, the men do not sing all of these songs. Women and girls can enjoy their unique way of Davenning.

Shabbos meals. Some families have separate tables for male and female guests at the Shabbos meals. A leading Rabbinical authority has said that a Mechitzah should be used when there are many Shabbos guests. Seating women together enables them to get to know each other and discuss topics that interest them. It also can prevent young boys and girls from becoming acquainted with each other when they are not yet ready for marriage – knowing each other at that stage serves no purpose and can cause negative consequences. If the men and women are in completely separate rooms and the men can't hear the women, the women can even sing, making the Shabbos meal more enjoyable.

Weddings. Separating the men and women at a wedding gives the couple a good start on their life together. The Rebbe King Moshiach Shlita emphasizes the importance of having a Mechitzah at a wedding – even when they are only eating and not only during the dancing. The women and girls can make the Kallah truly happy in special feminine ways. When all the women are together on one side they see the beautiful dresses of the family and other guests, uninterrupted by the uniform black and white of the men's suits. Women enjoy being part of this regal experience.

The Dancer

A young girl from a religious family had an exceptional talent for dancing. As she grew into a teenager, she began to dream of becoming a famous dancer and performing for large audiences. Although it is forbidden for a woman or girl to dance in front of men, she did not feel strongly enough about Yiddishkeit that this would deter her. She planned to make dancing her career when she would grow up.

One day a life-changing thought occurred to her. As she imagined herself dancing on stage in front of a mixed audience, she suddenly thought, "What if Moshiach were to come at that moment?" This made her reconsider her plans. She studied the teachings of Chabad Chassidus, which imbued in her a passion for religious observance.

She also found a positive way to channel her dancing talent: she directs girls in religious schools in their dances when they present shows for all-female audiences.